ABSTRACT

Maritime piracy has long-standing history throughout the world and, while tactics have changed, the basic criminal act and motives behind it have remained the same over time. Modern maritime pirate organizations are composed primarily of members of clans and tribes that operate as decentralized organizations and exhibit characteristics of complex adaptive systems. Understanding the behavior of these organizations will aid in the fight against maritime piracy. Connecting the behaviors of pirate organizations to complexity theory, or more specifically, complex adaptive systems, allows for the development of new approaches to combatting the problem of maritime piracy.

ACKNOWLEDGEMENT

Thank you to my thesis advisor, Professor Marlowe, for his time, patience, and dedicated mentoring throughout the process. Additionally, Captain Guiliani and Doctor Pavelec provided great insights and suggestions while building this product, and the Joint Forces Staff College's team of dedicated library professionals assisted tremendously in the research. Finally, my classmates in JAWS Seminar Three, as well as the rest of the students, faculty, and staff, made this year a tremendous learning experience.

DEDICATION

To my wife, children, family, and "Shipmates" everywhere.

TABLE OF CONTENTS

CHAPTER 1

Introduction: Why Maritime Piracy is a Problem

Over 70 percent of Earth's surface is water, and transportation by sea is the most economical and popular means of exchanging goods globally. Thousands of merchant ships, loaded with myriad types of cargo – from automobiles and other manufactured goods to coal and crude oil – ply the ocean each day destined for ports around the world. The global economy depends on sea routes to transport more than 90 percent of all trade. The growth of developing countries and the increase of free commerce throughout the world over the past several decades contributed to the rise in global sea trade from an estimated 2.566 billion tons in 1970 to 8.408 billion tons in 2008. Increases in technology and the world population's desire for more economical pricing continue to fuel maritime shipping as the predominant means of transporting goods. Furthermore, many countries lack their own capability to sustain the manufacturing of raw materials, fuel, and finished products, which necessitates those countries' need for long-term trade demands across the already busy sea trade routes. If the pace remains constant, some analysts believe the amount of goods transported by sea could increase to an estimated 23 billion tons by 2060.[1]

Given this dependence on global trade and the expectation that maritime shipping will continue to be the most economical means of transporting goods between world population centers, threats to maritime trade routes can lead to grave economic, social, and political impacts. The mere thought of the closure of the Suez Canal due to political

---

[1] Maritime Knowledge Centre, *International Shipping Facts and Figures - Information Resources on Trade, Safety, Security, Environment* (London, UK: International Maritime Organization, 2012), 7-8.

unrest in Egypt can lead to skyrocketing crude oil prices because of the increased distance required to sail around the Cape of Good Hope for bulk oil tankers to reach the Americas and Europe. Natural disasters precipitated by tsunamis, hurricanes, and typhoons can destroy large ports, block waterways, damage ships and, at a minimum, cause routing delays that lead to increased fuel consumption and delayed arrival dates, causing exorbitant increases in shipping costs. However, the uncertain, chaotic, and complex acts of maritime pirate organizations alone can achieve all of these effects and more.

Piracy Defined

Article 101 of the United Nations Convention on the Law of the Sea (UNCLOS) states:

> Piracy consists of any of the following acts:
> (a) any illegal acts of violence or detention, or any act of depredation, committed for private ends by the crew or the passengers of a private ship or a private aircraft, and directed:
> (i) on the high seas, against another ship or aircraft, or against persons or property on board such ship or aircraft;
> (ii) against a ship, aircraft, persons or property in a place outside the jurisdiction of any State;
> (b) any act of voluntary participation in the operation of a ship or of an aircraft with knowledge of facts making it a pirate ship or aircraft;
> (c) any act of inciting or of intentionally facilitating an act described in subparagraph (a) or (b).[2]

Since this international law excludes areas within a nation's territorial waters (12 nautical miles) and applies only to areas recognized as the "high seas," it does not consider the places most prone to the current maritime piracy threat (considered armed robbery by this

---

[2] United Nations, "United Nations Convention on the Law of the Sea," December 10, 1982, http://www.un.org/Depts/los/convention_agreements/texts/unclos/closindx.htm (accessed October 03, 2013), Article 101.

definition)[3]. The International Maritime Bureau (IMB) provides another useful definition of piracy, in that "Piracy is an act of boarding any vessel with the intent to commit theft or any other crime and with the intent or capability to use force in furtherance of that act."[4] This definition better serves what current counter-piracy efforts strive to resolve (maritime piracy on the high seas as well as within territorial sea limits), and it encompasses both of the United States Code Title 18 definitions of piracy on the high seas as well as robbery ashore. Section 1651 defines piracy under law of nations as, "Whoever, on the high seas, commits the crime of piracy as defined by the law of nations, and is afterward brought into or found in the United States, shall be imprisoned for life."[5] Section 1661 defines robbery ashore as, "Whoever, being engaged in any piratical cruise or enterprise, or being of the crew of any piratical vessel, lands from such vessel and commits robbery on shore is a pirate, and shall be imprisoned for life."[6]

For the purposes of this paper, maritime piracy encompasses the criminal acts of piracy on the high seas, piracy in territorial waters, and robbery ashore conducted from seagoing vessels, since these descriptions include the most commonly understood and contested forms of sea robbery.

Current Maritime Piracy Threat Regions

Maritime piracy has been a problem as long as ships have transported goods by sea. Early Greek records indicate battles against piracy in 694 B.C., and pirates

---

[3] Richard M. O'Meara, "Maritime Piracy in the 21st Century: A Short Course for US Policy Makers," *Journal of Global Change and Governance* 1, no. 1 (2007), 2, http://www.globalaffairsjournal.com/wp-content/uploads/2011/07/OMEARA.pdf (accessed October 03, 2013), 3.

[4] As quoted in Ibid., 3.

[5] U.S. Congress, *United States Code Title 18, Chapter 81*, (2012), 391.

[6] Ibid., 393.

kidnapped Julius Caesar in 75 B.C.[7] However, piracy has recently been the most

rampant in highly traveled sea routes near under-developed nations. Most notable of

these routes are adjacent to East Africa, West Africa, and Southeast Asia. The following

sections address the economic costs of maritime piracy in these regions; however,

economic costs are not the only price paid in the fight against this criminal activity. The

human costs, whether they are emotional, physical, or otherwise, also need consideration,

though they prove more difficult and impracticable to quantify since a dollar figure is

impossible to estimate in these circumstances. An example of these human costs includes

numerous reports of maritime pirates physically and psychologically abusing captured

seamen over the past several years. Additionally, on a per capita basis, assault and

hostage rates at sea off Somalia were higher in 2010 than on land.[8]

East Africa Maritime Piracy

In their most recent report, the Oceans Beyond Piracy (OBP) project estimated

Somali piracy alone cost the global economy an estimated $5.7-6.1 billion in 2012, even

after a decrease of an estimated 12.6 percent ($850 million) from 2011[9]. Cost estimates

were the greatest during the previous two years with 2010 estimated at $7-12 billion and

2011 estimated at $6.6-6.9 billion[10]. The three largest contributors to the overall price of

Somali piracy were the cost of security equipment and guards for merchant ships at $2.06

billion (up from $1.65 billion in 2011); the cost of increased speed used by merchant

---

[7] O'Meara, *Maritime Piracy in the 21st Century: A Short Course for US Policy Makers*, 2-8, 2.

[8] Martin N. Murphy, "Somali Piracy," *The RUSI Journal* 156, no. 6 (12/01; 2013/11, 2011), 4, http://dx.doi.org/10.1080/03071847.2011.642673 (accessed November 18, 2013), 8.

[9] Jonathan Bellish, *The Economic Cost of Somali Piracy 2012* (Denver, CO: Oceans Beyond Piracy, One Earth Future Foundation, 2013), www.oceansbeyondpiracy.org (accessed September 11, 2013), 1.

[10] Ibid., 7.

ships to evade attack at $1.53 billion (down from $2.7 billion in 2011); and the cost of military operations at $1.09 billion (down from $1.27 billion in 2011)[11]. The changes in cost appear to relate directly to the increase use of security measures and their inferred deterrence effect, the success of naval patrols, and a better appreciation of the high-risk areas by merchant ship captains and shipping companies.

Although the number of attempted pirate attacks off the coast of East Africa fell by 70 percent and the number of hijackings by 50 percent from 2011 to 2012 (due to the apparent reasons described above), the cost per successful hijacking rose from $250 million in 2011 to $421.4 million in 2012 because of the decreased number of hijackings[12]. While the current direct-action counter-piracy methods appear to be reducing the number of successful piratical acts, as evidenced by the dramatic decline in attempted hijackings from 2011 to 2012, the extremely high costs and effort employed by several disparate, global organizations and methods suggest the need for a new approach.

West Africa Maritime Piracy

While maritime piracy conducted by Somali-based groups appears to be on the decline with the ongoing counter-piracy efforts, West African piracy is on the rise, likely attributed to the inability of the Gulf of Guinea nations to police their waters and corrupt officials allowing piracy to happen. Additionally, the maritime shipping industries' focus on the East Africa maritime piracy problem probably diverted attention from the Gulf of Guinea. According to OBP, "The year 2012 marked the first time since the surge in piracy off the coast of Somalia that the reported number of both ships and seafarers

---

[11] Ibid., 14-24.

[12] Ibid., 7.

attacked in the Gulf of Guinea surpassed that of the Gulf of Aden and of the Western Indian Ocean."[13]

Unlike Somali pirates that generally hold ships for ransom as a means to make money, most pirate attacks in the Gulf of Guinea focus on the robbery of cargo, particularly refined petroleum products like gasoline. While the highest Somali attack ransom levied is believed to be $13.5 million (for a ship carrying $200 million in cargo), Murphy states that, "…gangs operating off Benin are believed to be taking two to three cargoes worth $5-10 million each month."[14] This seems to demonstrate a new business model for the pirates in the Gulf of Guinea when compared to those from Somalia. Furthermore, this model appears to have a more drastic economic impact since the pirate organizations are able to capitalize on the sale of stolen cargo more quickly than the ransom of cargoes or crew, without the overhead costs associated with holding ships for payment for months on end.

The reported number of attacks in the Gulf of Guinea in 2012 included 43 vessels (of which 83% included actual boardings, though speculation leads to the belief that unsuccessful attacks are underreported) and 966 seafarers[15], but historical metrics that define the economic cost of piracy in the Gulf of Guinea prove more difficult to quantify. In an initial attempt at quantification, OBP released a range of figures in an endeavor to measure the costs. For 2012, OBP estimated that the direct economic cost of West African piracy was between $674 million and $939 million. Of this, the greatest expense

---

[13] Kaija Hurlburt and D. Conor Seyle, *The Human Cost of Maritime Piracy 2012* (Denver, CO: Oceans Beyond Piracy, One Earth Future Foundation, 2013), www.oceansbeyondpiracy.org (accessed November 13, 2013), 12.

[14] Martin N. Murphy, "Petro-Piracy: Oil and Troubled Waters," *Orbis* 57, no. 3 (2013), 424, 434.

[15] Hurlburt and Seyle, *The Human Cost of Maritime Piracy 2012*, 13.

to the shipping industry was the cost of insurance, estimated from $358-427 million, while the cost to use private armed guards was $150 million. Even though the estimated price of stolen goods was only $34-101 million, the total cost of military expenditures to combat the threat was $100-150 million.[16] Additionally, OBP estimates the "indirect costs to affected industries in the billions of dollars."[17]

Southeast Asia Maritime Piracy

Even though no organization published statistics of the economic costs of maritime piracy in Southeast Asia as OBP did for the African regions, many useful statistics exist to help illustrate the problem of maritime piracy in this area. In its annual report for 2012, the International Maritime Organization (IMO) stated that the number of piracy and armed robbery incidents[18] occurring in the South China Sea dropped from 113 in 2011 to 90 in 2012. Conversely, the incidents occurring in the Strait of Malacca increased from 22 in 2011 to 24 in 2012.[19]

Raymond contends that, in the Strait of Malacca, the types of piracy conducted include, "robbery of vessels at sea, the hijacking of vessels, and kidnap-for-ransom attacks."[20] In the robbery attack, the amount of stolen goods typically ranges from $10,000 to $20,000. Hijacking that includes the seizure of the cargo may also include the seizure of the vessel for use or sale by the pirates. Furthermore, Raymond states that

---

[16] Ibid., 18-21.

[17] Ibid., 18.

[18] The IMO distinguishes between piracy taking place on the high seas and armed robbery occurring inport or at anchor, in accordance with the UNCLOS Article 101 definition and contrary to the IMB definition.

[19] International Maritime Organization, *Reports on Acts of Piracy and Armed Robbery Against Ships: Annual Report - 2012* (London, UK: International Maritime Organization, 2013), 1, 2.

[20] Catherine Z. Raymond, "Piracy and Armed Robbery in the Malacca Strait: A Problem Solved?" *Naval War College Review* 62, no. 3 (2009), 31, www.dtic.mil (accessed October 02, 2013), 33.

since 2001, kidnapping is the most serious type of piracy in the Strait of Malacca, and this type generally includes taking two or three senior crewmembers for ransom, usually demanded at $100,000 to $200,000 but more commonly negotiated to between $10,000 and $20,000.[21] However, more recent reports indicate that maritime piracy in the region may be experiencing an uptick in frequency, as well as a change in objectives, citing a November 2013 hijacking of a gasoil carrier whose full-cargo capacity estimates a net of more than $2.7 million. This same report also details the fear of increased insurance premiums for the shipping lines and the added expense this incurs.[22] The increased frequency, along with the changing objectives, are due likely to maritime piracy groups in this region attempting to define new methods to defeat current counter-piracy efforts of regional governments.

While finding no figures directly comparable to the Southeast Asia maritime piracy problem as with those available for East and West Africa, the information available concludes that maritime piracy throughout the world costs billions of dollars to combat, and organizations must continue to find more effective, economical means of dealing with and eradicating the threat.

Thesis Intent

Combatting maritime piracy is a struggle against decentralized organizations that present behaviors akin to self-organizing, complex adaptive systems. Using historical case studies and analysis of current operations, this thesis intends to link complexity theory and complex adaptive systems to the decentralized aspect of how pirate

---

[21] Ibid., 33-34.

[22] Keith Wallis, "Tanker Hijackings Raise Piracy Concerns in Seas Around Singapore," *Reuters*, November 12, 2013, http://www.reuters.com/article/2013/11/12/us-shipping-singapore-piracy-idUSBRE9AB06420131112 (accessed November 12, 2013).

organizations appear to operate. Based on the research, the paper will present recommendations that suggest a more effective means of viewing the problem. By considering the issue with a complex adaptive systems approach, and the understanding of how decentralized organizations function, Joint, Interagency, and Partner Nations will be able to provide the Combatant Commander a better understanding of how to fight maritime piracy in the modern world.

First, this thesis analyzes a case study of a historical problem region susceptible to maritime piracy. Next, a review of clans and tribalism, with focus on Somalia, serves as background by demonstrating the role tribalism played in the development of the recent East African piracy problem and how the role of tribalism in the insurgent-spawned civil war more than 20 years ago gave birth to the Somalia maritime piracy concerns of today. Additionally, an introduction to nonlinear theory, which includes chaos and complexity theories, will help form a new lens from which to observe and tackle the issue. The chapter also includes a discussion of decentralized organizations.

The objective of this thesis is to provide recommendations and inform the many organizations combatting maritime piracy around the world of different ways to view and combat the problem. The expectation is that the Combatant Commander can analyze maritime pirate organizations in a nonlinear, complex adaptive systems approach and away from the many current, linear approaches, thereby reducing the costs and effort involved in battling this ancient crime on the seas.

CHAPTER 2

The Barbary Coast – An Area Ripe for Piracy

An understanding of how maritime piracy organizations operate is important when attempting to combat the threat. This chapter briefly reviews the early history of the Barbary pirates to illustrate common threads on the motivations, means, and goals of maritime piracy organizations.

The Barbary States lined the northern coast of Africa and extended from the Atlantic Ocean west of the Strait of Gibraltar to Egypt, and the Mediterranean Sea comprised the majority of the shipping lanes; the historical Barbary States included Morocco, Algeria, Tunis, and Tripoli (the latter two with the modern day names of Tunisia and Libya, respectively). The Mediterranean coastal area of Morocco, Algeria, and Tunis were primarily rocky and high, while the coastal area of Tripoli was mainly low with reefs and shoal water extending well offshore. The coastal climate was mild with fertile land, and open harbors led into the Mediterranean to the north. The autumn and winter months produced strong winds throughout the Mediterranean, which presented hazards to sailing vessels.[1] As Allen states, "With its advantages of situation and climate, Barbary should have been a civilized and progressive country. Its Mohammedan population, however, consisting of Moors, Arabs, Berbers, Kabyles, and

---

[1] Gardner Weld Allen, *Our Navy and the Barbary Corsairs* (Hamden, CT: Archon Books, 1965), 1.

Turks, decided the character of the civilization."[2] Barbary was the given name of the region, based on the group of Berbers who inhabited the west.[3]

The leaders of the four Barbary States varied in title, but they were all under the governmental rule, at least to some extent, of the Grand Turk, or Sultan, in Istanbul, who also controlled Egypt. The Emperor, or Sheriff, ruled Morocco, the Dey led Algiers, the Bey governed Tunis, and the Pasha ruled Tripoli. None of the leaders came from royalty, though they considered themselves absolute monarchs because although they paid annual tributes to Istanbul, they showed little loyalty to the Sultan on Caliph otherwise. The leaders used the threat of death and violence as their power, and their governments were corrupt. Additionally, neither formal nor informal supportive agreements existed between the four rulers of the Barbary Coast.[4]

However, they cooperated on the control of the seas. As Chidsey writes, "…but in all matters pertaining to the shipping on the Mediterranean Sea they could be counted upon to act together. If one picked a certain victim, the others too fell upon him. If one issued privateering licenses like so many tax notices, the others were sure to follow."[5] The Barbary Coast rulers considered the Mediterranean their property and treated it as such, forcing the leading maritime nations of Europe to pay exorbitant tributes to each Barbary State individually, lest they face the wrath of the Barbary pirates, the corsairs[6].

---

[2] Ibid., 2.

[3] Donald Barr Chidsey, *The Wars in Barbary: Arab Piracy and the Birth of the United States Navy* (New York, NY: Crown Publishers, 1971), 6.

[4] Ibid., 2.

[5] Ibid., 6.

[6] Konstam explains that the term "corsair" in French means "privateer," and that the early actions of the Barbary corsairs more accurately describe privateering rather than piracy, since the corsairs acted under the authority of the Barbary rulers. He further states that "piracy" became a more appropriate term during the 17th and 18th centuries after the European nations "refused to recognize the authority of the

All nations considered the tributes paid to the Emperor, the Dey, the Bey, and the Pasha a less expensive form of protection than arming all of their merchant ships or sending their navies to patrol the Mediterranean and secure their national shipping, even though the annual tributes increased each year.[7] The ability of the Barbary States to cooperate in the control of the Mediterranean Sea and its shipping, with no formal or informal governing agreement between them and seemingly in a decentralized manner, illustrates the attributes of a complex adaptive system.

Origin and Methods of the Early Barbary Corsairs

After the Arabians inhabited the region during the seventh and eighth centuries and established Muslim control along the North African coast and extending into Spain and Sicily[8], dynasties ruled the Barbary Coast beginning in the ninth century, with some of them lasting several hundred years[9]. However, as Konstam writes, "Although these vast territories were united by religion, there was little or no political unity, and the fragmentation of the Almohad dynasties resulted in a string of petty chiefdoms dotted along the African coast from Morocco to Libya."[10]

Even though changes in empires throughout the years led to periods of increased turmoil, "…the rule of these African princes was generally mild and enlightened."[11] Most of the princes were Berbers who tolerated Christianity and worked together without

---

Barbary rulers." Angus Konstam, *Piracy: The Complete History* (Oxford, UK: Osprey Publishing, 2008), 76. For the purposes of this paper, the term "corsair" applies to the pirates from the Barbary Coast.

[7] Chidsey, *The Wars in Barbary: Arab Piracy and the Birth of the United States Navy*, 6.

[8] Konstam, *Piracy: The Complete History*, 75.

[9] Stanley Lane-Poole and J. D. Jerrold Kelley, *The Barbary Corsairs* (Westport, CT: Negro Universities Press, 1970), 21.

[10] Konstam, *Piracy: The Complete History*, 75.

[11] Lane-Poole and Kelley, *The Barbary Corsairs*, 22.

religious bias. During this period, the Barbary States and European countries maintained amicable relations, each relying on the other for trade, which produced reciprocal treaties and the exchange of diplomats.[12] Although various, yet seemingly insignificant, conflicts arose between Barbary and Europe beginning in the early eleventh century, "…in succeeding centuries, under more settled governments, war became very rare, and mutual amity was the prevailing policy."[13]

Although prohibited by the treaties signed between the Barbary and European states, non-state sanctioned piracy still existed, mainly by European Christians up until the fourteenth century. The increased size of the commercial fleets brought a downturn of European piracy, but it also produced a greater reliance on sea robbing income for the African Muslims. Unable to control the swell of the early maritime piracy organizations, the great and relatively peaceful Barbary dynasties – with their well-run governments but little armed force capability – faltered and created a haven from which rampant piracy began to take hold.[14] By the fifteenth and sixteenth centuries, the local rulers throughout Barbary encouraged the corsairs to use their ports, which injected great wealth to the local economy, in exchange for a percentage of the profits gained from the sale of slaves and plunder[15].

While both Christian and Muslim piracy existed much earlier, the beginning of the sixteenth century included war between the Muslims and Christians, as well as commencing a period of about 300 years of maritime piracy dominance by the Barbary

---

[12] Ibid., 22-23.

[13] Ibid., 24.

[14] Ibid., 24-27.

[15] Konstam, *Piracy: The Complete History*, 75.

corsairs. This era resulted from the 1492 invasion of Granada by Ferdinand and Isabella, forcing thousands of expelled Spanish Moor refugees to North Africa and the Barbary Coast. Understandably, the expatriated Moors harbored much hatred toward the conquering Spanish and reciprocated the wrongdoing by waging piratical attacks on Spain using their knowledge of the Spanish coast.[16] Other than simple retaliation against Spain, the primary purpose of the early attacks by Moorish pirates was to rescue the remaining Moors living in the coastal region from the brutality suffered at the hands of the Spanish, with looting taking place as a convenience of location[17]. In general, the Europeans viewed the corsairs as "cruel and fanatical Muslims, who waged an undeclared war against their religious enemies" even though many of the corsairs were Christian to Islam converts, and "Renegade Christians made up a substantial portion of corsair numbers."[18] Maritime piracy conducted by the Barbary corsairs grew quickly from the early stages of reciprocity against the Spanish and blossomed into a way of life.

The Barbary corsairs generally made three cruises each year, constrained by the Mediterranean weather and their small, but fast and heavily manned boats. The general mode of operation was for single vessel assaults on unsuspecting and lightly armed merchant shipping, using early operational deception techniques, such as a few European-dressed crewmembers in plain view, while the others lay below waiting for the consummation of the attack.[19] Once alongside their prey, the rest of the crew appeared, "...a terrible multitude springing up it seemed from nowhere, their eyes flashing, mouths

---

[16] Allen, *Our Navy and the Barbary Corsairs*, 2-3; and Lane-Poole and Kelley, *The Barbary Corsairs*, 8.

[17] Chidsey, *The Wars in Barbary: Arab Piracy and the Birth of the United States Navy*, 11.

[18] Konstam, *Piracy: The Complete History*, 78.

[19] Chidsey, *The Wars in Barbary: Arab Piracy and the Birth of the United States Navy*, 7.

open in horrid screams, while they brandished their scimitars."[20] If there was resistance from the other vessel or the attack was not effective on the first attempt, the corsairs usually gave up and sailed away in search of another victim[21]. The small, fast boat attack tactics, as well as the lack of persistent attacks against a resisting merchant ship, remain common traits of modern maritime pirates.

The corsairs, after seizing and looting the victim vessel, imprisoned the crew as slaves. In those days, the slaves captured at sea and returned to the corsairs' bases were predominantly white European Christians.[22] Pressed directly into the service of the corsairs themselves, many slaves became oarsmen on the pirates' boats. The largest of the pirate boats, or galleys, used as many as 270 oarsmen, termed "galley slaves." Chained to benches and forced to row for more than ten hours, the galley slaves suffering from exhaustion were of no use to the pirates and often discarded overboard.[23] The corsairs sold the remaining slaves at auction, or they became labor for public projects in the home countries of the pirates. Ransoming slaves was also a possibility, though the prices sought were high, few relatives could afford to pay them, and the lengthy and complex bargaining system often-stymied negotiations.[24]

During the seventeenth century, the corsairs increased their opportunity from the sea by conducting a greater number of raids inland against the European nations, venturing ever further north and reaching as far as the North Sea, looting villages, and imprisoning their inhabitants for ransom back to their families. The corsairs' wealth

---

[20] Ibid., 7.

[21] Ibid., 7.

[22] Ibid., 8.

[23] Allen, *Our Navy and the Barbary Corsairs*, 8-9.

[24] Chidsey, *The Wars in Barbary: Arab Piracy and the Birth of the United States Navy*, 9.

increased because of the profits incurred from the looting and ransoms, thus swelling the pirates' insatiable desire for more revenue.[25] Money from ransom negotiations remains one of the greatest sources of income for modern day maritime piracy organizations, and its negotiation process appears no less complex and lengthy now then it was during the time of the Barbary corsairs.

Early Barbary Corsair Leaders

Originating from the island of Lesbos with a long history of producing pirates[26], the Barbarossa brothers, Arouj and Kheyr-ed-Din, were the first of the vaunted corsair leaders. They were of neither Arabian nor Turkish decent, but their Albanian-born father converted to Islam, though their mother was a Christian.[27] Arouj became a pirate boat captain but found himself constrained by the Turkish Sultan's naval fleet. Desiring increased opportunity as a member of an eastern Mediterranean pirate gang, Arouj thus made his way to the Barbary Coast, creating his first base in Tunis in the early sixteenth century.[28] He secured the Tunis Bey's cooperation by promising him one-fifth of the plunder, for which Arouj received free use of the ports and protection from pursuit.[29] Arouj made his first major conquest as a corsair leader in 1505 by capturing two ships flying the flag of Pope Julius II. After a hard fight, he seized the cargo-laden trading ship along with her warship escort and returned both to Tunis, securing his reputation as a great corsair.[30]

---

[25] Allen, *Our Navy and the Barbary Corsairs.*, 6-7.

[26] Lane-Poole and Kelley, *The Barbary Corsairs*, 31.

[27] Chidsey, *The Wars in Barbary: Arab Piracy and the Birth of the United States Navy*, 11.

[28] Lane-Poole and Kelley, *The Barbary Corsairs*, 32.

[29] Ibid., 35.

[30] Konstam, *Piracy: The Complete History*, 81.

Arouj soon made his way into Algiers and set-up the same 20 percent arrangement with the Dey. However, this was subsequently reduced to ten percent and then to nothing, since the Dey of Algiers was afraid to protest. Eventually, Arouj murdered the Dey and became the ruler of Algiers, keeping the entire lot of his pirate bounty for himself.[31] His reign did not last long when finally, in 1517, Arouj died in battle with the Spanish army sent to Algiers by King Charles V to rid the region of the corsair infestation.[32]

Kheyr-ed-Din succeeded his brother as the Dey of Algiers and leader of the Barbary corsairs, and the Turkish Sultan made him the overall ruler of the rest of the Barbary Coast. He became a military leader for the Sultan and fended off a Spanish assault of Algiers. His base now secure, he attacked other Christian targets over the next several years, making raids along southern France and attacking Spanish shipping. He continued his conquest by venturing to other spots in the Mediterranean, including raids into Spain and battles with Christian fleets, until 1545, when he retired to Turkey and placed his son in charge of Algiers and the corsairs. He died the next year.[33] The Barbarossa brothers, "…saved the Barbary coast from the Spanish invaders, and helped ensure that these fragile semi-independent city-states would survive long after their passing. In the process they established a fearsome reputation for the Barbary corsairs they commanded, which would last for more than a century."[34]

---

[31] Chidsey, *The Wars in Barbary: Arab Piracy and the Birth of the United States Navy*, 13.

[32] Lane-Poole and Kelley, *The Barbary Corsairs*, 51-52.

[33] Konstam, *Piracy: The Complete History*, 83-86.

[34] Ibid., 86.

There were several other leaders of the corsairs after the Barbarossa brothers ruled, but "Probably the last and perhaps the greatest Barbary corsair was Murat Rais, who rose to prominence during the second half of the 16th century."[35] Born in Albania, he began his leadership of the corsairs in 1574 and resumed attacks on the Spanish in an undeclared war for the next two decades. The Turkish Sultan made Murat his admiral in 1594, and he subsequently led a large assault into southern Italy. He remained the Sultan's commander on the seas against Christian targets while keeping the Muslim trade traffic secure. He died in 1638 leading an Ottoman attack into his native Albania, which began the decline of the great Barbary corsair leaders.[36]

The End of the Barbary Corsair Era

Beginning in the mid-seventeenth century, several European nations led attacks on the Barbary Coast in attempts to rid the Mediterranean of the corsair problem and protect their merchant shipping. However, the corsairs continued to fight back[37], and the piracy problem persisted into the eighteenth century when many countries in Europe began the practice of paying tributes to the Barbary States to protect their shipping. No longer falling under the British umbrella of protection after gaining independence, United States merchant trade came under attack.[38] Tributes paid by foreign nations overcame revenue from slave trade as the Barbary States' primary source of income in the eighteenth century[39].

---

[35] Ibid., 89.

[36] Ibid., 89-90.

[37] Ibid., 93.

[38] Chidsey, *The Wars in Barbary: Arab Piracy and the Birth of the United States Navy*, 21-22.

[39] Konstam, *Piracy: The Complete History*, 94.

United States flagged merchant shipping quickly became targets of the Barbary

pirates. The government negotiated a trade agreement with Morocco, but not the other

Barbary States, and Americans began appearing in the slave markets. Attacks on United

States shipping by the Barbary pirates continued until President Thomas Jefferson sent

the United States Navy and Marines to Tripoli in 1801. After numerous battles over the

next several years, Tripoli agreed to a peace treaty in 1805 and returned all American

slaves for $60,000, as well as ensuring free passage for merchant shipping.[40]

The downfall of the Barbary States began in 1815 when the United States, Britain,

and France allied in a second clash against the pirate haven, culminating with the

bombardment of Algiers in 1816. As a result, Algiers agreed to cease enslaving

Christians. Algiers and Tunis subsequently became French colonies, and Tripoli fell

under the Ottoman Empire until 1911, when it became an Italian colony.[41]

Barbary Summary

The Barbary corsairs were a menace to international shipping throughout their

tenure. While governments offered some sort of organization – and logically offered the

argument of legitimized privateering on behalf of somewhat sovereign nations – the

corsairs acted on their own in pursuit of money and dominance. Even though they also

engaged in wars of aggression as a pseudo-military force on behalf of their city-states, the

countless acts of piracy remain the preeminent feature in their history. The ransoming of

their captured slaves and marketing of the stolen goods define their existence in the

annals of maritime crime.

---

[40] Ibid., 94.

[41] Ibid., 94.

Although not structured predominantly along tribal or clan lines and consisting of a mixture of religious and cultural backgrounds, the ability of the Barbary corsairs to function under a very loose and decentralized organization construct aligns with similar maritime piracy organizations in existence today. The following chapter reviews the origin of the Somali maritime piracy issue now plaguing the East African coast and its direct ties to tribalism and clans. Like the Barbary States, Somalia operates under a weak government that cannot control the maritime piracy problem yet provides enough legitimacy and organizational protection to allow piracy to flourish as a way of life.

CHAPTER 3

Tribal Influences on Somali Maritime Piracy and Insurgency

Maritime piracy disrupts commerce and trade around the globe, causing lost revenue and increased costs for the shipping companies to avoid and combat the threat, as well as increased shipping insurance costs. Insurgencies around the world consume precious resources as legitimate governments struggle and fight insurgencies in support of political legitimacy. While neither all-inclusive nor intended to over-generalize, maritime piracy and insurgency organizations often have much in common. Many of these organizations are born out of an oft forgotten form of governance: tribalism or clans. Several of those fighting the war against maritime piracy, as well as insurgency, neglect to consider the important role that tribalism and clans play in the irregular warfare scenarios of recent history.

A common thread among maritime piracy and insurgencies are the ideologies of each group that rebel against a government, or spawn because of the lack of formal government. Human nature tends to thrive on organization; when the organization is not working or leaves a vacuum, the leaders of non-state organizations rally their followers toward a common goal that either leads to their survival or furthers their beliefs. In either event, the complexity of the organization strives to achieve a state of routine governance and equilibrium. Consequently, piracy and insurgency networks likely return to their tribal or clan roots to attain equilibrium and exist because of a failed or weak nation-state, or as a means of rebellion against the government in power.

Strong, organized, and legitimate governments possess the ability to provide the support required for and desired by the inhabitants, such as law enforcement, health care, education systems, and economic opportunity. Without support from the government, the population seeks other means to provide for their needs and desires, which could include illegitimate activities such as maritime piracy. Therefore, governments that provide opportunities to their populace and possess the means to enforce laws can curb the tendencies toward criminal acts as a source of income. This chapter will discuss key tribal[1] components of maritime piracy and insurgency organizations by examining recent historical accounts of each in Somalia. An overview of these accounts will help to understand better the history as well as the current situation. Additionally, parallels exist between the weak governments of the Barbary States and Somalia that led their populations to turn toward maritime piracy as a means of living.

A Brief History of Somalia and the Clans

The roots of maritime piracy off the East African coast and the Horn of Africa are distinguishable in the ethnic region that consists of roughly eight million Somali people[2]. Somalis converted to Islam and traced their Arab lineage to the Prophet Muhammad after establishing a history of trade with the Arabian Peninsula more than a thousand years ago. In the north, the port of Zeila became a hub for trade with the Arabians, along with

---

[1] The terms "tribe" and "clan," along with their derivatives, are interchangeable in this paper. In general, a clan is a subset of a tribe or "sub-tribe," normally based on family ties. Conversely, a tribe may consist of many family organizations or clans. Regardless of the different nuances of the terms, the use of them in this chapter is to demonstrate how this form of non-state governance influences maritime piracy and insurgency organizations.

[2] Iona M. Lewis, *Understanding Somalia and Somaliland: Culture, History, Society* (New York, NY: Columbia University Press, 2008), 1.

Mogadishu in the south.[3] An estimated 60 to 70 percent of Somalis are of pastoral nomadic descent, though many of those live in populated cities and only maintain nominal nomadic ties. The smaller population near the coast relies on commerce and fishing to subsist.[4]

Somalia consists of six major divisions or clans, with each lineage tracing back to ancient Arabian descent. Near the southern coastal regions, though predominantly centered west of Mogadishu in the fertile areas between two rivers (the Shebelle and the Juba), are the Digil and Rahanweyn clans, who are farmers. In the northern regions, albeit with a smaller presence in the southern inland areas, are the Dir, Isaq, Hawiye, and Darod clans. The Darod clan is the largest and most dispersed clan of the six.[5]

During the nineteenth century, France, Great Britain, and Italy sought to stake claim to territories in Africa, but the boundaries set by the Europeans did not take clan and tribal lands into consideration. After resolving their territorial claims subsequent to the opening of the Suez Canal in 1869, the French territory included Djibouti, while the British controlled the northeast corner of the Horn of Africa, and the Italians ruled the southern part of Somalia, which included Mogadishu. However, the new boundaries still did not consider the clan territories with the Islamic Somali clans divided between Kenya, Ethiopia, and Somalia.[6] The British and Italians granted independence to their territories in the 1950s, and the Somalis established a national government in Mogadishu to rule the current boundaries of Somalia. However, "…clans and sub-clans were not ready for rule

---

[3] Ibid., 1-2.

[4] Ibid., 3.

[5] Ibid., 3-5.

[6] Lester H. Brune, *The United States and Post-Cold War Interventions: Bush and Clinton in Somalia, Haiti, and Bosnia, 1992-1998* (Claremont, CA: Regina Books, 1999), 13-14.

by a central government. Somalia's inter-clan relations had local ethical rules but lacked an overarching concept of law essential to a modern civilized nation."[7]

In 1969, a military coup, led by General Mohammed Siad Barre and backed by the Soviet Union, ousted the Somali president. During the Cold War, both of the Superpowers, striving to gain influence in the region, provided military and economic assistance to the Barre regime. In the 1970s, Barre led a war with Ethiopia to claim the province of Ogaden, which included Somali clans that had been under Ethiopian control since the nineteenth century. The war opened against a United States-backed Ethiopian regime, though a Soviet-backed rebel later overthrew the Ethiopian government. Forfeiting the war and leaving Ogaden under Ethiopian control after encountering strengthened Soviet-backed troops against his forces, Barre began receiving assistance from the United States and other groups. As a result, the United States replaced the Soviet Union as the influencer in Somalia in 1980.[8]

Incensed by the corruption of the Barre government, which wasted much of the northern clans' economic income from the export of their livestock, the Somalia National Movement (SNM), led by the Isaq clan (who later led the establishment of Somaliland), began attacking towns in the north during the first part of 1988. Barre countered these attacks with military action that destroyed several Isaq towns and killed 5,000 people. The United States ceased its relief actions, and the SNM continued the uprising while attempting to incite the support of other clans.[9] Insurgent rebels eventually overthrew Barre after increased unrest in January 1991, but after uniting for his ousting, "at least

---

[7] Ibid., 14.

[8] Ibid., 14.

[9] Ibid., 15.

thirteen clans and sub-clans fought for regional or national control."[10] Following the collapse of the nation of Somalia, an estimated two million members of this population became refugees in neighboring African countries, the Middle East, North America, and Europe[11].

Because each of the clans tend to maintain their distinct cultural and genealogical ties, it becomes easy to understand the difficulty of forming a united central government in the country. However, in 1991, the Isaq clan, along with components of the other clans in the northern region, compromised and formed the Somaliland Republic under the leadership of clan elders. A popular movement to become their own nation independent from the south, with which they garnered much anger and distrust, fueled this desire for secession.[12] Following the creation of Somaliland, in 1998 a group called the "Harti Confederacy," consisting of elders from three sub-clans of the Darod, created the Puntland State of Somalia to increase solidarity within the region and claim territory within Somalia. This was done out of fear from the Isaq clan's territorial claim and dominance in Somaliland, as well as the Hawiye clan's control of Mogadishu and continued positioning to extend their influence further into south-central Somalia. Puntland officially intended to join a future reunited state of Somalia, and therefore, did not declare full independence like Somaliland.[13]

---

[10] Ibid., 16.

[11] Lewis, *Understanding Somalia and Somaliland: Culture, History, Society*, 1.

[12] Ibid., 75.

[13] Jay Bahadur, *The Pirates of Somalia: Inside their Hidden World* (New York, NY: Pantheon Books, 2011), 28-29.

Clan Ties to East African Maritime Piracy

This lack of formal governance throughout Somalia, along with the incessant internal clan strife and high poverty levels, became the breeding ground for the most recent history of domineering pirates throughout the East African coastline. While piracy entered the Somali scene soon after the insurgent-led civil war, due to the fall of the central government and lack of means to assert law and order, Puntland-based pirates began to make their biggest gains in the mid-2000s. Early piratical acts stayed close to the shore and focused mainly on fishing trawlers and other small vessels.[14]

Even then, many of these acts were more indicative of privateering, as the Puntland government sanctioned a local lobster fishing owner to "end illegal fishing by foreign fleets" off the coast in 1993. Known as one of the pioneers of piracy in Somalia, the leader of this effort, Abdiwahid Mahamed Hersi ("Joaar"), intended to form a coast guard for the state of Puntland. However, according to Joaar, southern warlords sanctioned many of the illegal fishing ships that he had been seizing, and as a result, the warlords began to threaten him for hijacking the ships under their protection, and he therefore soon ceased this line of work.[15] These threats underscore the importance of understanding the clashes between the clans of Somalia and the internal strife that tribalism caused on the increased number of attacks, as well as the bigger ransoms sought, by competing clans along the Somali coast for control of the seas that developed from the mid-1990's and continue through today.

A year or two after Joaar's coast guard began (1994 or 1995, depending on the account) fishermen from the coastal Puntland city of Eyl began operations against illegal

---

[14] Ibid., 30.

[15] Ibid., 31.

fishing trawlers and created their own piracy groups within a sub-clan of the Darod, the Majerteen[16]. Though their methods and area of attacks remained basic, still operating mainly within the coastal waters of Puntland, Bahadur suggests that these fishermen provided "the original models for the oft-invoked media image of the fisherman-pirate locked in a one-sided struggle against the forces of foreign exploitation."[17] This group appears to have remained aligned along clan lines and within the boundaries of the yet-to-be fledgling "state" of Puntland while not venturing far from the coast.

However, inter-clan cooperation can exist in maritime piracy. Farther down the coast of Somalia, Mohamed Abdi Hassan, known as Afweyne ("Big Mouth"), formed the "Somali Marines" in the city of Haradheere. This coastal city, about halfway between Eyl and Mogadishu, is within the Hawiye clan area, and Big Mouth organized his pirate group from within the Hawiye sub-clan of the Habir Gedir. While he recruited mainly from within his own clan, Big Mouth relied on the expertise of the Eyl pirates and brought them onboard to train his group. This initial training relationship morphed into a cooperative that eventually led to collaborative piracy efforts between the Habir Gedir and Majerteen pirates. Additionally, Bahadur credits Big Mouth as the first pirate to recognize the full business potential of piracy, which even included the solicitation of investors to fund his organization.[18]

Whether or not this inter-clan cooperation still exists today (based on the traditional clashes between the various Somali clans, the answer is likely "no"), Big Mouth is no longer in the piracy business but is now in a Belgian prison awaiting trial for

---

[16] Ibid., 32-33.

[17] Ibid., 32.

[18] Ibid., 32-33.

hijacking a Belgian ship in 2009. After arriving in Belgium – lured there to act as an advisor for a film about maritime piracy – police arrested and charged him and one of his accomplices with piracy, organized crime, and kidnapping.[19] He could be sentenced to 30 years in prison for hostage taking, along with another 15 years for piracy, if found guilty[20].

In 2008, five primary pirate bases existed in Somalia, according to the International Experts Group, all aligned based on clan divisions. In Eyl and Garad, sub-clans from the Darod clan maintain their bases, and sub-clans of the Hawiye clan occupy Hoboyo, Haradheere, and Mogadishu pirate camps.[21] The long-standing tribal influences in Somalia directly affect and enable maritime piracy, and clan governance plays a large role in determining the success or failure of the pirate gangs. Even though the international community attempted to instill a sense of national government over the entire nation of Somalia throughout the years, the clan distinction of these five pirate bases suggests that a government that does not consider clan peculiarities will not prosper and have little effect on reducing or eliminating maritime piracy originating from Somalia.

---

[19] Philippe Siuberski, "Belgium Traps Somali Pirate Chief with Lure of Stardom," *AFP*, October 14, 2013 http://www.google.com/hostednews/afp/article/ALeqM5jx46hDhhqoSG46hLjPrpGK3HeQzw?hl=en (accessed October 15, 2013).

[20] James M. Bridger, "The Rise and Fall of Somalia's Pirate King: And the Reverse-*Argo* Sting that Bagged Him," *Foreign Policy*, November 04, 2013, http://www.foreignpolicy.com/articles/2013/11/04/the_rise_and_fall_of_somalia_s_pirate_king (accessed November 05, 2013).

[21] Martin N. Murphy, *Somalia: The New Barbary? Piracy and Islam in the Horn of Africa* (New York, NY: Columbia University Press, 2011), 92.

Clan Ties to the Insurgency-Bred Civil War in Somalia

Just before the pirate gangs in the northern half of Somalia were gaining strength, the United States found itself in the midst of strife in Mogadishu when the United Nations embarked on a mission to ensure food delivery to the drought-stricken region and its starving people. The United States soon found itself embroiled in the midst of an insurgency-turned-civil war as different clans wrestled for control of the country.

After Barre and his followers fled Somalia for Ethiopia and Kenya, Mohamed Farah Aideed and Mohamed Ali Mahdi – two of the leaders in the overthrow of the Barre regime – became competitors who attempted to shape Somalia. Their warring factions tore Mogadishu apart and caused massive civilian strife. The United Nations, seeking to end the infighting, brought Aideed and Mahdi to the negotiating table, which ended in a cease-fire agreement in March 1992, followed by the establishment of the United Nations Operation in Somalia (UNOSOM) after the adoption of United Nations Security Council Resolution (UNSCR) 751.[22] Hindered by incessant bickering between its officials, the disjointed United Nations organization lacked the ability to integrate various Non-Governmental Organizations (NGOs) sending aid to Somalia. The United Nations' organization proved unable to provide and sustain relief fast enough. Additionally, United Nations bureaucratic decisions to send additional troops to Somalia, which led to perceptions of bias and preference of Mahdi over the rest of the clan leaders, outraged the other Somali leaders and began the further distancing of Aideed and his supporters, the largest following of all the groups. Aideed proclaimed that the United Nations was the enemy of Somalia, and heavy fighting against peacekeeping troops erupted in November

---

[22] Brune, *The United States and Post-Cold War Interventions: Bush and Clinton in Somalia, Haiti, and Bosnia, 1992-1998*, 17.

1992. Even the clan followers of Mahdi joined in the outrage against the United Nations.[23]

Looking to play a larger role in providing aid for the crisis in Somalia, the United States led a multinational United Task Force (UNITAF) stemming from UNSCR 794, "...to establish protective conditions for humanitarian aid to reach Somalia's starving people."[24] Even though UNITAF established a limited safe area centered on Mogadishu for the various relief organizations to operate and eventually save an estimated 100,000 Somalis, the security diminished when UNOSOM II replaced UNITAF[25]. Furthermore, with only enough troops to secure distribution points into and out of Mogadishu, clans continued to fight for control in other parts of Somalia. Aideed, Mahdi, and other leaders maintained their influence throughout the region, though held in check under the threat from UNITAF forces. However, neither of the UNOSOMs had enough troops to control the clans.[26] Finally, in an attempt by the United Nations to establish a national government in Somalia, two reconciliation conferences were held in Addis Ababa, Ethiopia, with the second one leading to an agreement signed by 15 clan leaders in March 1993 that extended the previous cease-fire agreement and ratified a Transitional National Council (TNC). This agreement, however, rapidly fell by the wayside when UNITAF forces departed in May 1993.[27]

UNITAF's assertion that security reigned throughout Somalia and that warfare by the clans no longer existed led to the withdrawal of the preponderance of United States

---

[23] Ibid., 17-19.

[24] Ibid., 21.

[25] Ibid., 23.

[26] Ibid., 24.

[27] Ibid., 25-27.

forces and established UNOSOM II in May 1993 by adoption of UNSCR 814[28]. Forces

under UNITAF numbered 37,000, while UNOSOM II contained only 14,000, later rising

to 28,000. Aideed quickly rebelled against the UNOSOM II commander, and the

downfall began.[29] Aideed's followers ambushed Pakistani troops in June 1993 killing

two dozen, and UNSCR 837 led to UNOSOM II's focus "...on the hunt for Aideed to

punish the most powerful group in Mogadishu."[30] This and other attacks led to a build-

up of United States forces and the infamous "Blackhawk Down" battle in October 1993

while searching for Aideed[31]. American public angst led to the withdrawal of all United

States forces by March 1994, and the remaining UNOSOM II forces left by March 1995.

Aideed proclaimed himself president, though Mahdi and Osman Hassan Ali (Atto)

opposed this assertion. Their forces, comprised of five sub-clans, wounded Aideed in a

firefight in July 1996, and he subsequently died in surgery.[32]

Major General Thomas Montgomery, commander of United States forces in

Somalia, explained the difficulties in establishing a unified Somali government by

describing three competing circles of influence: clans, political groups, and tribalism.

First, there were six major clans and numerous sub-clans, with the clan agenda competing

with the national agenda. Second, six major political groups existed that aligned along

clan affiliation, with no single political group dominating militarily, and no political

group with national appeal. Finally, tribal influences placed individual and family needs

over all others, strained limited resources within the country, and produced a short-term

---

[28] Ibid., 27.

[29] Ibid., 28-29.

[30] Ibid., 30.

[31] Ibid., 32.

[32] Ibid., 33.

outlook versus long-term goals that caused constant friction and confrontation among various groups.[33]

Somali Tribalism Summary

A country that once enjoyed steady income from fishing and agriculture fell apart because of the insurgency-spawned civil war, leading to a nation devoid of a legitimate national government able to protect its interests. Somalia's failed national government, later replaced in part by weak regional governments, helped permit maritime piracy to take root in the early 1990s by not possessing the means to enforce law and order. The maritime piracy groups, based along clan ties and backed by local tribal governance, bound together for their common good and started the "business" of maritime piracy by initially practicing regional government-sanctioned privateering. The inability of the weak government to control the privateering with legitimate law enforcement allowed privateering to morph into full-blown maritime piracy practiced around the Horn of Africa in recent years. Lacking any other meaningful income, maritime piracy enjoyed prominence among many clan-based groups. These clans need to work together now to reverse this trend and establish legitimized trade through strong government; the formation of the Somaliland government demonstrated that cross-clan cooperation is possible.

Tribalism and clans play crucial roles in developing governments and restoring order in strife-riven nations by providing legitimacy to governmental formation. Zeman astutely observes, "In these chaotic environments, it is often the unity and strength

---

[33] LTG(ret) Thomas Montgomery, "U.S. Intervention in Somalia '92-'94" (presentation to Joint Advanced Warfighting School, Joint Forces Staff College, Norfolk, VA, October 28, 2013).

provided by the tribe that allows for security and survival."[34] Clans must work together

to establish governments capable of running a nation and establishing law. The Somalia

maritime piracy issue will not resolve itself until the restoration of law and order on land

is complete. Additionally, the rival clans must agree to a common form of governance

for a country devoid of such for over 20 years, which led to the insurgencies beginning in

the late 1980s that became the breeding ground for the maritime piracy issue faced in

East Africa today.

The insurgent-led collapse of the Barre regime, which left a void of an all-

encompassing government for the entire nation-state of Somalia, led to other problems as

well, particularly the welcoming atmosphere for terrorist groups like Al Shabab, believed

to maintain ties with Al Qaeda. Some authors argue that the Sharia law imposed by the

Islamist terrorists tends to weed-out piracy, due to the animosity created by the profits

sought by pirate organizations competing with the fundamental tenets of Islam[35]. Others

indicate that there is a direct connection between Somali maritime piracy organizations

and the terrorist group by citing reports that Al Shabab receives at least part of its funding

from the pirate organizations[36]. Furthermore, if Al Shabab does maintain ties to Al

Qaeda, particularly the primarily Yemen-based Al Qaeda in the Arabian Peninsula

(AQAP), the speculation of joint operations between the two groups to conduct terrorism

against maritime shipping in the region has potentially grave consequences[37].

---

[34] Phillip M. Zeman, "Tribalism and Terror," *Small Wars & Insurgencies* 20, no. 3-4 (2009), 681 (accessed August 12, 2013), 681.

[35] Currun Singh, "Al Shabab Fights the Pirates," *New York Times*, October 23, 2013, http://www.nytimes.com/2013/10/23/opinion/international/al-shabab-fights-the-pirates.html?_r=0; (accessed October 31, 2013).

[36] Murphy, *Somali Piracy*, 4-11, 6.

[37] Ibid., 6.

Regardless of the connection between the Somali-based maritime pirate clans and the Al Shabab terrorist organization based there, the relative non-governance of Somalia leads to instability within its borders that can breed instability outside of its borders. However, Peters has a much dimmer view, stating "…the majority of Islamic states…are going to continue to grow relatively (and some absolutely) poorer, as prospects falter and populations increase."[38]

The successful, though struggling, government of Somaliland is an example of clans beginning to work together to reach a common goal. The involvement of many clan elders to attain a central government in that area proved at least somewhat successful in the early developmental stages with low instances of maritime piracy in the region. When addressing the self-made success in Somaliland resulting from inter-clan peace conferences versus the failure of the United Nations' efforts elsewhere in the country, Lewis writes,

> This is not the place to conduct a detailed comparison of these inexpensive and low profile Somaliland peace conferences with their extremely expensive, high profile counterparts in Somalia. Here it is simply enough to say that, in general, the former were successful while the latter failed dismally. Of the many factors involved, a crucial difference here is clearly the dominant role played in Somaliland by the local authorities, the 'stake-holders' in the pompous jargon of developers.[39]

To restore governance and order in Somalia and thus aid in the eradication of maritime piracy in the region, an understanding of tribalism and clans is required. Imposing the will of outside agendas alone and in a vacuum does not work. The failed government of Somalia led directly to the onslaught of maritime piracy throughout the

---

[38] Ralph Peters, "The New Warrior Class Revisited," *Small Wars & Insurgencies* 13, no. 2 (08/01; 2013/10, 2002), 16, http://dx.doi.org/10.1080/09592310208559178 (accessed October 31, 2013), 23.

[39] Lewis, *Understanding Somalia and Somaliland: Culture, History, Society*, 95.

region. While tribalism and clans may not be the root cause of the issue, the inability, for the most part, of the clans to cooperate for the greater good of their nation and build a united government continues to exacerbate the problem. Either the clans must come together on their own accord to restore governance, as in the case of Somaliland, or outside entities, whether it is individual nations or a coalition of states under the United Nations, must understand the clan tensions and idiosyncrasies to assist in nation building. Convincing the Somali population that good governance will create opportunity is an area for international governments, the United Nations, and NGOs to address cooperatively.

In addition to understanding the intricacies of tribalism in attempts to rebuild the nation, a greater understanding of the nonlinear organization of the maritime piracy groups and an appreciation for complexity theory and the characteristics of decentralized organizations is in order. Until a government of Somalia emerges, capable of policing itself and enforcing law and order in the region, this understanding of the nonlinear functioning groups needs to occur concurrently with nation building to allow organizations combatting the maritime piracy threat to counter it effectively.

CHAPTER 4

Organizational Theory Background

Historically, the military, as well as most governmental and Non-Governmental

Organizations (NGOs), viewed the problem of combatting maritime piracy in a linear

sense. For example, the various international navies involved in coalition and allied

operations in-and-around the pirate-infested waters of Somalia most often use direct-

action operations to deter piracy. These operations include responding to reported pirate

attacks from merchant ships in attempts to disrupt an attack in progress, or in cases in

which the piratical act was successful, in direct-action attempts to remove the pirates

from the vessel. In other cases, direct-action operations by naval forces to deter pirate

mother ships from leaving the safety of shore-based pirate camps to conduct operations

of piracy offshore include mostly deterrence by presence near the pirate camps,

attempting to prevent the mother ships with their striking skiffs from escaping to do

action. While these activities have been successful in recent history and helped in the

decrease in numbers of successful attacks, non-linear operations garnered much of the

credit, and rightly so.[1]

Examples of non-linear operations of deterrence include the IMO-recommended

Best Management Practices (BMP) like razor wire, water spray, evasive maneuvering,

safe muster points, and fortified citadels[2]. Another asymmetric form of protection

---

[1] The knowledge of the employment of the types of counter-piracy operations described here are from the author's experiences in command of USS BAINBRIDGE (DDG 96) gained during a counter-piracy deployment to the Gulf of Aden, Indian Ocean, and North Arabian Sea in support of NATO's Operation OCEAN SHIELD in 2011.

[2] International Chamber of Shipping, *BMP4: Best Management Practices for Protection Against Somalia Based Piracy* (Edinburgh, Scotland, UK: Witherby Publishing Group Limited, 2011), 23-37.

employed by many merchant ships transiting high-risk areas is the use of Private Security Companies (PSCs), which are armed guards contracted by the shipping lines[3]. While these PSCs provide direct-action measures to thwart maritime pirate attacks, this asymmetric solution, as Murphy points out, "…is about the privatisation of naval force" since nation states either do not have the means to provide military protection and escorts for their merchant shipping, or they are reluctant to do so[4]. While no merchant vessel employing an armed detachment has been successfully captured[5], the use of force (or threat of force) and BMP actions alone is not enough to combat the maritime piracy threat. Understanding and viewing the organizations of maritime pirates themselves non-linearly, instead of the current view by most groups as being military-like, centralized organizations, will aid in combatting the threat.

This chapter includes descriptions for background and understanding of chaos and complexity theories, along with a discussion of the characteristics of decentralized organizations, which support the organizational analysis of maritime piracy. Viewing maritime pirate organizations in this way enables organizations charged with fighting maritime piracy a different way to approach the problem and derive alternative solutions for combatting the threat.

Chaos Theory

The word "chaos" invokes images of many different things, and most of those present a situation that contains a high degree of disorder. However, chaos theory, a relatively new scientific mathematical discipline, presents a way to view systems in a

---

[3] Murphy, *Somali Piracy*, 4-11, 8.

[4] Ibid., 8.

[5] Ibid., 8.

nonlinear, and often more useful and more truthful, sense. In one of the most well-known

and classical examples of chaos theory, Lorenz posed the notion that a butterfly flapping

its wings in Brazil could cause an ensuing tornado in Texas, otherwise known as the

"Butterfly Effect"[6]. The reality of that question, as unlikely that its actual action will

result, nevertheless provides a good descriptor of the things that chaos theory attempt to

explain. Seemingly unrelated and independent events can interact with each other to

produce nonlinear results not easily understood or explained. Whereas linear systems

provide a known and predictable outcome, nonlinear systems do not necessarily. While

some researchers tend to look at these types of events as random occurrences, the

interactions of individual components bind the behaviors of chaotic systems to produce a

range of outcomes, thus possessing at least some degree of predictability.

James describes chaos theory as, "…a specific range of irregular behaviors in

systems that move or change."[7] He further states that a chaotic system must be bounded,

nonlinear, non-periodic, sensitive to small disturbances, and mixing, and that without one

of these characteristics, the system cannot be chaotic, but that if it does contain all of

these, the system "…can be driven into chaos."[8]

While chaotic systems in general are very difficult to solve, one can predict the

outcome for short-term periods. By understanding these short-term results and the

influences on them, inference of long-term system trends is possible.[9] Furthermore, by

considering long-term trends, as well as by controlling or manipulating the influential

---

[6] Edward N. Lorenz, *The Essence of Chaos* (Seattle, WA: University of Washington Press, 1995), 181.

[7] Glenn E. James, *Chaos Theory: The Essentials for Military Applications*, 10th ed. (Newport, RI: Naval War College, Center for Naval Warfare Studies, 1996), 3.

[8] Ibid., 38.

[9] Ibid., 65.

variables within a chaotic system, one can potentially change the outcome of the system or move it toward stability[10]. While it is impossible to change a massively chaotic system such as weather patterns (at least at the present time), analysis proves useful when applied to maritime piracy organizations and ways to influence their behavior.

A basic understanding of chaos theory, along with the knowledge of being able to predict and control the variables of a chaotic system, is an important component of the following sections on complexity theory. Chaos theory provides a foundation for understanding the development of complexity theory.

Complexity Theory

Imagine vehicular traffic on a crowded Interstate highway (the system) in a busy metropolitan area just prior to rush hour. The system has a set of physical bounds (the guardrails and physical medians) and a set of starting parameters (speed limit, other laws, and the initial flow of low-volume traffic). While not affected as much during the low traffic periods outside of rush hour times, as traffic density increases, small perturbations within the system can cause large disturbances to the flow of traffic. Examples of some of these perturbations to the system could include a car with a flat tire, a driver distracted while texting that swerves into the next lane of traffic, or a slow-moving truck merging from an on-ramp.

These seemingly simple, unrelated, and unpredictable events, even appearing chaotic in nature, by independent entities within the system, can change the flow of traffic and disrupt the commute. Behaviors emerge from the interacting entities (the drivers and their vehicles), and unpredictable patterns can result. The reactions by a

---

[10] Ibid., 70.

driver behind a vehicle that just lost control can cause that driver to swerve left or right, which then influences the reactions of the driver to whichever side he swerved, and so on. When a truck several hundred yards ahead of another driver applies its brakes, the car behind it may apply its brakes, and a series of brake lights ripples down the highway, causing an unpredictable set of reactions and potentially decreasing the speeds unnecessarily of other vehicles for as long as the trend continues. The same sorts of reactions, along with the effects on the other independent entities acting on each other within the system, are felt when a speeding driver suddenly slows when he sees a police car ahead, or when a rubber-necker slows down to gain the optimal view of an accident or breakdown on the shoulder.

These types of independent reactions by individual entities, along with other unrelated events (like a downed signpost or ladder that fell off a truck and landed in the middle of the travel lane) tend to lead to disorder within the system. Yet the experience levels of most drivers, as well as the initial set of bounds and parameters imposed on the system, overcome these perturbations, and the system self-organizes to compensate, maintaining the flow of traffic, albeit at decreased speed and output, to achieve the objective of continuing down the highway to the final exit and arrival at the destination.

The example above provides useful insight into the ideas of complexity theory and describes many of its elements. Complexity theory encompasses complex adaptive systems comprised of independent agents or groups of agents that present self-organizing, self-adapting, and emergent behavior properties. It also incorporates chaos theory and uses this as a basis to understand the development of complexity theory and how complex adaptive systems work, as well as how changing a set of initial conditions, within bounds placed upon the system, help explain how the system functions and evolves. Complexity theory is a relatively new science, having come of age only about 30 years ago, and applies to economic, physical, ecological, sociological, biological, and myriad other types of systems. As a common example used to aid in understanding complexity theory, Kauffman and others describe emergent behavior, one of the baseline properties associated with complexity theory, with the statement, "The whole is greater than the sum of its parts."[11]

Waldrop explains how complexity theory developed out of chaos theory by stating, "…chaos theory has shaken science to its foundations with the realization that very simple dynamical rules can give rise to extraordinary behavior…yet chaos itself doesn't explain the structure, the coherence, the self-organizing cohesiveness of complex systems."[12] Taking this a step further, the "edge of chaos" is where complexity resides. In other words, the edge of chaos is the place that complex systems have the capability of balancing chaos with order. "The edge of chaos is the constantly shifting battle zone between stagnation and anarchy, the one place where a complex system can be spontaneous, adaptive, and alive."[13]

This basic understanding of the interconnection between chaos and complexity, their differences from ordered and random systems, and their potential to incorporate ordered and random systems in their self-adaptation, is fundamental when attempting to explain the actions of maritime piracy organizations. In other words, the traditional way

---

[11] Stuart Kauffman, *At Home in the Universe: The Search for the Laws of Self-Organization and Complexity* (New York, NY: Oxford University Press, 1996), 24.

[12] M. Mitchell Waldrop, *Complexity: The Emerging Science at the Edge of Order and Chaos* (New York, NY: Simon & Schuster, 1992), 12.

[13] Ibid., 12.

of viewing maritime piracy organizations (many of which maintain ties to tribalism and clans, as described in the previous chapter) as linear, military-like organizations does not work, and instead we must view them through the lens of a complex adaptive system.

Complex Adaptive Systems

As discussed, complexity theory encompasses the study of Complex Adaptive Systems (CAS) and is a means of viewing the interactions and structure of highly complicated organizations, groups, and systems. Holland describes CAS as "...systems that have a large numbers of components, often called agents, that interact and adapt or learn."[14] Moreover, he maintains that they contain four primary features, including parallelism (large numbers of agents simultaneously sending and receiving signals); conditional action (agent actions depend on received signals, often viewed as the conditional "if/then" formation of statements or rules); modularity (the ability of the agents to react to a given situation by sequencing rules together); and adaptation and evolution (the agents change over time by adapting to improve performance, not by random variations).[15]

These four features of CAS apply to the previous example of the Interstate highway system. Parallelism describes the large number of vehicles on the highway, each sending signals to the other drivers by their speed, direction of travel, brake lights, and others not as obvious, such as watching a loosely held ladder in a truck ahead and changing lanes to avoid the impending doom of it falling. Conditional action represents a driver's actions based on the signals received from the other vehicles and the surrounding

---

[14] John H. Holland, "Studying Complex Adaptive Systems," *Journal of Systems Science and Complexity* 19, no. 1 (2006), 1, 1.

[15] Ibid., 1-2.

environment. Modularity equates to a driver who performs a sequence of actions based on the situation, such as braking and then changing lanes to avoid a suddenly decelerating vehicle ahead. Finally, adaptation and evolution exist in the highway example by the experience gained by drivers operating in non-ideal situations (like poor weather) and applying that new knowledge level the next time they encounter a similar scenario. Adaptation and evolution also apply to the scenario of drivers able to self-organize themselves in the highway system to overcome the impediment of a break down in the center lane, yet still maintain the ability to re-route and continue to their destination.

The interaction of many agents within a CAS lends to the requirement of studying these systems by nonlinear means. Holland contends that the conditional rules (the if/then statements) employed by agents in a CAS do not allow easy approximation using linear techniques. Furthermore, the rules employed by the agents change, and the agents themselves rarely attain a steady state, always adapting to the new situation.[16] He continues by stating, "Add to this that agents are continually revising and updating their information, much as with the regular updates used in weather prediction. As a result chaotic effects are only occasionally influential."[17] (Note here the inferred reference to Lorenz' "Butterfly Effect" in chaos theory.) Referring back to the "whole is greater than the sum of its parts" theorem described earlier, the study of CAS, therefore, requires the consideration of the interactions of the agents in addition to the summing of the parts to provide better analysis[18].

---

[16] Ibid., 3.

[17] Ibid., 3.

[18] Ibid., 3.

Holland also discusses three properties as opportunities for understanding and controlling CAS. First, he describes "lever points," which are instances within a CAS where a small input or intervention (a shock to the system) can lead to a prolonged effect directed at a specific change[19]. Next, he describes the notion that CAS "...have a hierarchical organization of boundaries enclosing boundaries, with signals that are attuned to those boundaries" and those boundaries establish individual histories[20]. His third property of CAS is that they "...evolve in an open-ended fashion, wherein an initially simple system exhibits increasing diversity of interaction and signaling."[21]

Referring back to the Interstate highway analogy, the "lever points" could equate to inserting a zone of decreased speed limits, much like speed restrictions posed while traveling in a construction area. The second property (boundaries enclosing boundaries) is a parallel to a highway with speed limit signs, further enforced by highway troopers on patrol or mounted speed cameras; the individual histories develop from whether or not a driver receives a speeding ticket from bad practices, which then influences future driver behavior, at least temporarily. Lastly, the third property of a simple system exhibiting increased diversity describes the point where traffic patterns and driver behaviors evolve from areas of low-density traffic to those of metropolitan rush hour complexity, e.g. entering a bustling city with a high-density traffic pattern from relatively benign driving behavior in the rural outskirts of the city.

Advancements in computing technology and speed over the past several decades enabled an increased capability to study chaos and complexity theories. While computers

---

[19] Ibid., 6.

[20] Ibid., 6.

[21] Ibid., 6.

provide a more effective means to examine the intricacies of CAS and thus provide a useful technique that increases knowledge in these studies, Holland warns "…exploratory computer-executable models define possibilities not actualities."[22] Computer models allow for understanding the interactions, but do not fully predict the actions, since the agents will interact with each other based on a small set of rules, even though almost endless possibilities of outcomes still abound. He summarizes this very important point by stating,

> Even simple mechanisms with simple interactions can generate complex behavior. Consider again chess or Go: Fewer than a dozen rules – the counterpart of defining mechanisms – generate a system with perpetual novelty. After hundreds of years of study we still find new patterns and strategies for playing these games. For a cas the rules that define the agents' behavior are the equivalent of the rules of the game.[23]

Complexity theory, therefore, is one piece of the puzzle to identifying the interactions of maritime piracy organizations. By applying the features and properties of Complex Adaptive Systems, as well as understanding the general concepts of emergent behavior, self-organization, and self-adaptation of a system of agents working from a simple rule set, groups that are working to combat and eradicate the lawless acts of maritime piracy can envision new ways in which to view these criminal organizations. By looking at those groups in this light, and understanding that not every complex adaptive system or maritime piracy organization's actions are fully predictable, at least an understanding of the rules of the organization can exist, which leads to greater knowledge and improved ways of dealing with the threat.

---

[22] Ibid., 3.

[23] Ibid., 3.

Decentralized Organizations

The notion of decentralized (or leaderless) organizations gained prominence in a wide-variety of circles over the past several years with the publication of *The Starfish and the Spider: The Unstoppable Power of Leaderless Organizations*. In fact, the book garnered success within the United States military by its inclusion in the 2012 version of the Chairman of the Joint Chiefs of Staff reading list. As the analogy of the book's title illustrates, viewing a centralized organization as a spider implies that if the head of the spider is cut-off, the spider will die. Likewise, in decentralized organizations, a starfish has neither a head nor a centralized governing section that is in control. Continuing this, if a leg of the starfish is cut-off, that leg will generate another independent starfish, and the original starfish will produce a replacement leg.[24] "The absence of structure, leadership, and formal organization, once considered a weakness, has become a major asset. Seemingly chaotic groups have challenged and defeated established institutions. The rules of the game have changed."[25] Understanding these new rules is necessary in the fight against maritime piracy, and the increasing prominence of the concept of decentralized organizations, used in conjunction with the previous discussion of Complex Adaptive Systems features and properties, offers some insight into how these organizations operate.

Brafman and Beckstrom describe a decentralized organization as one that contains no hierarchy, no headquarters, and no clear leader. While a leader can emerge in a decentralized organization, the most he can do is influence others in the organization by

---

[24] Ori Brafman and Rod A. Beckstrom, *The Starfish and the Spider: The Unstoppable Power of Leaderless Organizations* (New York, NY: Portfolio, Penguin Group, 2007), 34-35.

[25] Ibid., 7.

his actions. However, they are clear in distinguishing that an "open" system such as this is not analogous to anarchy; rules and normal behaviors abide as policed by the other members of the organization.[26] Moreover, when a centralized organization attempts to attack a decentralized organization, "a decentralized organization tends to become even more open and decentralized."[27] As seen in the previous examples of maritime piracy organizations, while the groups or tribes may have leaders or elders, they are more influential in their roles rather than the command and control roles of centralized organizations, bound simply by the rules of the game and not the rules of the rulers. Furthermore, it is the pressure and influence of others within those organizations that enforce the rules rather than an autocratic power at the top of the organization imposing heavy-handed leadership.

Decentralized organizations tend to stand on five characteristics, or five legs of the starfish; while not needing all five legs to survive, these organizations tend to work best when all are present[28]. First, these organizations consist of non-hierarchical circles of members (communities) that share the same tradition and heritage, but each independent circle maintains its own distinct habits and norms[29]. Second, the decentralized organization needs a catalyst, or a "person who initiates a circle and then fades away into the background."[30] Third, the organization must possess a shared ideology that motivates the members of the circles and unites them to respect each

---

[26] Ibid., 19-20.

[27] Ibid., 21.

[28] Ibid., 87.

[29] Ibid., 88.

[30] Ibid., 92.

47

member's contributions[31]. Fourth, a decentralized organization starts from a preexisting network of people that form the circles and share the same ideology[32]. Finally, a decentralized organization requires a champion that advertises and spreads the group's ideals or goals[33].

Brafman and Beckstrom equate Al Qaeda to a decentralized organization by having independent circles around the globe, operating on the same ideology and networks, with the original catalyst being Osama bin Laden[34]. Extending that logic, Osama bin Laden arguably became the champion for the organization when his role as original catalyst was complete. Furthermore, as with Barbary and Somalia maritime piracy, Al Qaeda thrives mainly in areas with weak governance.

Crawford and Miscik term leaders that seem to operate best in fledgling governments as "mezzanine rulers." They claim, "Governments across the Middle East and South Asia are increasingly losing power to substate actors as those actors insert themselves at a mezzanine level of rule between the government and the people."[35] Additionally, the local publics' regard these leaders as "championing ethnic, religious, or political causes,"[36] which is indicative of groups driven by ideology and is a characteristic of decentralized organizations. Therefore, mezzanine rulers could perform the initial role of a catalyst in a decentralized organization, then fade into the background or become the champion of the organization, much like Osama bin Laden.

---

[31] Ibid., 94-95.

[32] Ibid., 96.

[33] Ibid., 99.

[34] Ibid., 140.

[35] Michael Crawford and Jami Miscik, "The Rise of the Mezzanine Rulers: The New Frontier for International Law," *Foreign Affairs* 89, no. 6 (2010), 123, 123.

[36] Ibid., 123.

To combat or challenge decentralized organizations, one method is to change their ideology. Since eliminating all catalysts and circles within this type of organization is nearly impossible, defeating or changing the ideology, the cohesive goals that hold the organization together, has a tremendous effect on defeating the organization but takes a long time.[37] The next method to combat the decentralized organization is to centralize it by injecting a mechanism that creates a level of authority, thereby creating an organization of hierarchy[38]. The third way of defeating a decentralized organization, as suggested by Brafman and Beckstrom, is to decentralize one's own organization and become a catalyst for smaller circles to combat the enemy's circles at the same level[39]. This final approach appears most conducive to combat the maritime piracy threat.

Organizational Theory Summary

Understanding the theory of the structure and interactions of these types of systems is paramount for organizations working to eliminate the threat of maritime piracy and offers alternative ways to comprehend and deal with these criminals. Additionally, increased understanding of nonlinear thinking allows one to view problems in a different way and not look solely at the simple "cause and effect" or linear interpretation of the problem.

For instance, understanding where the lever points (opportunities for influence) of a CAS exist allows organizations charged with fighting the crime of maritime piracy an opportunity to affect the outcome or behavior of maritime piracy organizations. An

---

[37] Brafman and Beckstrom, *The Starfish and the Spider: The Unstoppable Power of Leaderless Organizations*, 144.

[38] Ibid., 152.

[39] Ibid., 155.

example of a lever point for a maritime piracy organization could be with the clan elders for the region. By influencing the clan elders, whether by offering an alternative form of income for those clan members participating either in or most likely to look toward maritime piracy for their livelihood, or by some sort of coercion to compel the elders to crack down on maritime piracy in the region, various nonlinear solutions to the problem of maritime piracy exist.

Another instance of understanding CAS in countering maritime piracy includes the use of BMP. By seeking trends and commonalities among the Somali piratical acts, the IMO recommended successful actions to deter maritime pirate attacks on merchant ships sailing near Somalia. Unlikely that the BMP spawned directly from complexity theory understanding, the IMO nevertheless was able to find ways to influence the outcomes of the CAS by studying the trends and find at least some degree of predictability in the maritime pirates' operating procedures. Further study of the trends in West Africa maritime piracy should prove useful in helping to overcome the problem in that region.

Finally, understanding the workings of decentralized organizations will also aid in defeating maritime piracy, most likely in finding ways to influence the catalysts of these organizations. Influencing the catalysts' views or ideologies, whether by offering alternative methods for income or some sort of coercion as in the lever points example above, can lead to positive change in the organization toward the desired direction of the groups attempting to counter the threat.

CHAPTER 5

Conclusions and Recommendations

This thesis reviewed the requirement for innovative solutions to combat the maritime piracy threat by examining the need for continued counter-piracy operations. Understanding the definition of maritime piracy, along with an appreciation of the economic and human costs associated with current means of fighting the crime, underpin the need for new approaches. The review of the origins and methods used by the Barbary corsairs and Somali pirates provides a means to draw similarities from historical and current case studies of maritime piracy organizations, including the role that tribal tendencies play into the conduct of the organizations. Finally, the overview of complex adaptive systems and decentralized organizations offers a different way to view maritime piracy organizations and presents alternative solutions to the problem.

Conclusions

Maritime piracy organizations appear to operate best from nations where a weak, although not completely non-existent, government exists. The Barbary States provide an early example of this, where even though piracy existed by the permission of and benefit for the Barbary rulers through taxes paid to them by the corsairs, the rulers of these states did not possess the capability to completely control the corsair problem and legitimize maritime trade. More recently, the Somali piracy issue thrived under the loose federation of tribal government, particularly in Puntland, where local law enforcement efforts are insufficient to combat the criminal activity. Government corruption in both of these cases exacerbated the problem. The rise in maritime piracy in the Gulf of Guinea over the past several years points to yet another example of weak governments that either do not have the capability or possess the desire (due to corruption) to eliminate the havoc caused by sea robbers. Therefore, maritime piracy seems to thrive under the regimes of fledgling, though not completely failed, nations.

In many respects, mezzanine rulers appear to fit the mode of ideological catalysts or champions found within a decentralized organization, and they operate in the void between weak governments and the people of those nations. A significant characteristic of weak state governments that attracts the mezzanine rulers to those countries and allows them to flourish is that, "Under current international law, the government…remains accountable for all actions, including those of mezzanine rulers, within the territory over which it has sovereignty."[1] In other words, the nations from which organizations – criminal or otherwise – operate are accountable for crimes committed by those organizations.

Disregarding international law by foreign intrusions ashore brought the defeat of the Barbary corsairs, and in some instances hampered the success of the Somali pirates. However, the fact remains that host nations are responsible for the actions of their inhabitants, and those nations that are unable or unwilling to enforce international law allow maritime piracy to exist in places like East and West Africa today. In today's society, foreign military intervention even in weak states is nearly unpalatable and rarely used unless in response to a direct threat, as is the case with the United States' reluctance to operate military forces on the ground in Somalia.

---

[1] Crawford and Miscik, "The Rise of the Mezzanine Rulers: The New Frontier for International Law," 129.

While maritime piracy has always been and remains a business, mezzanine rulers play a significant role in its success by their influence as catalysts or champions for the maritime piracy organizations. Therefore, understanding complex adaptive systems and decentralized organization theory offers other ways of dealing with these mezzanine rulers without necessarily resorting to the use of direct military intervention.

Recommendations

Overwhelming force via military kinetic operations is an option to eradicate maritime piracy; however, the economic costs and risks involved to troops and civilians, along with the world population's current negative opinion toward the use of military force for policing actions, are prohibitive. Using complex adaptive systems and decentralized organization theory provides useful insights to other avenues to analyze and combat the threat posed by maritime piracy and its organizations. This section presents several recommendations for United States military leadership, as well as those of the Inter-Agencies and Partner Nations, to consider when conducting counter-piracy operations.

While creating a realistic model of complex adaptive systems is difficult since those types of systems are nearly unpredictable, an analysis of trends and key parameters capable of influence will provide additional means to combat the success of maritime piracy organizations. For example, the influencing of key tribal or clan leaders to cease their support of maritime piracy through various means such as presenting them alternative forms of income will affect the indigenous support enjoyed by leaders of pirate gangs. In addition, analyzing the pirate's trends, tactics, and areas in which they operate provides a way to invoke nonlinear defenses, such as the Best Management Practices previously described.

In countries with weak governments, engagement of the "mezzanine rulers" to persuade them toward the desired outcome is imperative. To alleviate the concern of undermining their authority, working alongside the weak governments while incorporating the views of the mezzanine rulers will enhance the government's status and legitimacy. Greater legitimacy will lead to that nation's enjoyment of increased cooperation from foreign nations by demonstrating the ability to secure maritime trade throughout the region.

One of the ways to defeat a decentralized organization is to decentralize one's own organization and become a catalyst for smaller circles within the other organization, influencing that larger organization in the direction it goes. Accomplishing this takes time and ingenuity, however. Similar to the above example of influencing key tribal leaders, by influencing smaller groups within the decentralized organization, other outcomes are attainable. As an example, offering legitimate sources of income to groups of individuals involved in maritime piracy gangs or likely recruits for those gangs will dissuade those individuals from piracy as an occupation. Non-Governmental Organizations (NGOs) are particularly well equipped to conduct training and funding for occupations such as farming, livestock husbandry, fishing, and other legitimate business trades.

Finally, while several Professional Military Education courses teach chaos and complexity theories as part of their curricula, in most cases, this is simply a broad brush of the topic embedded in the middle of the lectures of great military theorists such as Carl von Clausewitz and Sun Tzu. However, through further analysis of their works, a thorough demonstration of the nonlinear understanding the great military theorists possessed is realized, specifically as evidenced by Clausewitz' referral to "friction" and the "fog of war." To create a deeper level of intellectual understanding of nonlinear thinking, service colleges should devote additional time in their curricula to this type of study. A greater understanding, particularly of complexity theory, allows senior leaders to view problems outside of the simple "cause-effect" linear lens. Development of a recommended curriculum to teach nonlinear thinking to senior and future leaders is an area suitable for further research.

BIBLIOGRAPHY

Allen, Gardner Weld. *Our Navy and the Barbary Corsairs.* Hamden, CT: Archon Books, 1965.

Bahadur, Jay. *The Pirates of Somalia: Inside their Hidden World.* New York, NY: Pantheon Books, 2011.

Bellish, Jonathan. *The Economic Cost of Somali Piracy 2012.* Denver, CO: Oceans Beyond Piracy, One Earth Future Foundation, 2013, www.oceansbeyondpiracy.org (accessed September 11, 2013).

Brafman, Ori and Rod A. Beckstrom. *The Starfish and the Spider: The Unstoppable Power of Leaderless Organizations.* New York, NY: Portfolio, Penguin Group, 2007.

Bridger, James M. "The Rise and Fall of Somalia's Pirate King: And the Reverse-*Argo* Sting that Bagged Him." *Foreign Policy.* November 04, 2013. http://www.foreignpolicy.com/articles/2013/11/04/the_rise_and_fall_of_somal ia_s_pirate_king (accessed November 05, 2013).

Brune, Lester H. *The United States and Post-Cold War Interventions: Bush and Clinton in Somalia, Haiti, and Bosnia, 1992-199*8. Claremont, CA: Regina Books, 1999.

Chidsey, Donald Barr. *The Wars in Barbary: Arab Piracy and the Birth of the United States Nav*y. New York, NY: Crown Publishers, 1971.

Crawford, Michael and Jami Miscik. "The Rise of the Mezzanine Rulers: The New Frontier for International Law." *Foreign Affairs* 89, no. 6 (2010): 123-32.

Holland, John H. "Studying Complex Adaptive Systems." *Journal of Systems Science and Complexity* 19, no. 1 (2006): 1-8.

Hurlburt, Kaija and D. Conor Seyle. *The Human Cost of Maritime Piracy 2012.* Denver, CO: Oceans Beyond Piracy, One Earth Future Foundation, 2013, www.oceansbeyondpiracy.org (accessed November 13, 2013).

International Chamber of Shipping. *BMP4: Best Management Practices for Protection Against Somalia Based Pirac*y. Edinburgh, Scotland, UK: Witherby Publishing Group Limited, 2011.

International Maritime Organization. *Reports on Acts of Piracy and Armed Robbery Against Ships: Annual Report - 2012.* London, UK: International Maritime Organization, 2013.

James, Glenn E. *Chaos Theory: The Essentials for Military Applications*. The Newport Papers. 10th ed. Newport, RI: Naval War College, Center for Naval Warfare Studies, 1996.

Kauffman, Stuart. *At Home in the Universe: The Search for the Laws of Self-Organization and Complexity*. New York, NY: Oxford University Press, 1996.

Konstam, Angus. *Piracy: The Complete History*. Oxford, UK: Osprey Publishing, 2008.

Lane-Poole, Stanley and J. D. Jerrold Kelley. *The Barbary Corsairs*. Westport, CT: Negro Universities Press, 1970.

Lewis, Iona M. *Understanding Somalia and Somaliland: Culture, History, Society*. New York, NY: Columbia University Press, 2008.

Lorenz, Edward N. *The Essence of Chaos*. Seattle, WA: University of Washington Press, 1995.

Maritime Knowledge Centre. *International Shipping Facts and Figures - Information Resources on Trade, Safety, Security, Environment*. London, UK: International Maritime Organization, 2012.

Montgomery, Thomas. "U.S. Intervention in Somalia '92-'94." Presentation to Joint Advanced Warfighting School, Joint Forces Staff College, Norfolk, VA, October 28, 2013.

Murphy, Martin N. "Petro-Piracy: Oil and Troubled Waters." *Orbis* 57, no. 3 (2013): 424-37.

———. *Somalia: The New Barbary? Piracy and Islam in the Horn of Africa*. New York, NY: Columbia University Press, 2011.

Murphy, Martin N. "Somali Piracy." *The RUSI Journal* 156, no. 6 (12/01; 2013/11, 2011): 4-11, http://dx.doi.org/10.1080/03071847.2011.642673 (accessed November 18, 2013).

O'Meara, Richard M. "Maritime Piracy in the 21st Century: A Short Course for US Policy Makers." *Journal of Global Change and Governance* 1, no. 1 (2007): 2-8, http://www.globalaffairsjournal.com/wp-content/uploads/2011/07/OMEARA.pdf (accessed October 03, 2013).

Peters, Ralph. "The New Warrior Class Revisited." *Small Wars & Insurgencies* 13, no. 2 (08/01; 2013/10, 2002): 16-25, http://dx.doi.org/10.1080/09592310208559178 (accessed October 31, 2013).

Raymond, Catherine Z. "Piracy and Armed Robbery in the Malacca Strait: A Problem Solved?" *Naval War College Review* 62, no. 3 (2009): 31-42, www.dtic.mil (accessed October 02, 2013).

Singh, Currun. "Al Shabab Fights the Pirates." *New York Times*, October 23, 2013, http://www.nytimes.com/2013/10/23/opinion/international/al-shabab-fights-the-pirates.html?_r=0; (accessed October 31, 2013).

Siuberski, Philippe. "Belgium Traps Somali Pirate Chief with Lure of Stardom." *AFP*, October 14, 2013, http://www.google.com/hostednews/afp/article/ALeqM5jx46hDhhqoSG46hLj PrpGK3HeQzw?hl=en (accessed October 15, 2013).

U.S. Congress. *United States Code Title 18, Chapter 81,* 2012.

United Nations. "United Nations Convention on the Law of the Sea." December 10, 1982. http://www.un.org/Depts/los/convention_agreements/texts/unclos/closindx.ht m (accessed October 03, 2013).

Waldrop, M. Mitchell. *Complexity: The Emerging Science at the Edge of Order and Chaos.* New York, NY: Simon & Schuster, 1992.

Wallis, Keith. "Tanker Hijackings Raise Piracy Concerns in Seas Around Singapore." *Reuters,* November 12, 2013, http://www.reuters.com/article/2013/11/12/us-shipping-singapore-piracy-idUSBRE9AB06420131112 (accessed November 12, 2013).

Zeman, Phillip M. "Tribalism and Terror." *Small Wars & Insurgencies* 20, no. 3-4 (2009): 681-709 (accessed August 12, 2013).

Suggested additional readings:

Beyerchen, Alan. "Clausewitz, Nonlinearity, and the Unpredictability of War." *International Security* 17, no. 3 (Winter, 1992): 59-90, http://www.jstor.org/stable/2539130.

Bird, Miles T. "Social Piracy in Colonial and Contemporary Southeast Asia." BA, Claremont McKenna College, 2013. In Google, http://scholarship.claremont.edu/cmc_theses/691 (accessed October 02, 2013).

Boot, Max. "Pirates, then and Now: How Piracy was Defeated in the Past and can be again." *Foreign Affairs* 88, no. 4 (July/August, 2009): 94-107, http://www.jstor.org/stable/20699624 (accessed November 26, 2013).

Bruton, Bronwyn E. *Somalia: A New Approach.* New York, NY: Center for Preventive Action, Council on Foreign Relations, 2010.

Crawford, Michael and Jami Miscik. "The Rise of the Mezzanine Rulers: The New Frontier for International Law." *Foreign Affairs* 89, no. 6 (November, 2010): 123-32, http://ezproxy6.ndu.edu/login?url=http://search.ebscohost.com/login.aspx?direct=true&db=ofs&AN=504497262&site=ehost-live&scope=site (accessed December 04, 2013).

Daniels, Christopher L. *Somali Piracy and Terrorism in the Horn of Africa.* Lanham, MD: Scarecrow Press, 2012.

Dunigan, Molly, Dick Hoffmann, and Peter Chalk. *Characterizing and Exploring the Implications of Maritime Irregular Warfare.* Santa Monica, CA: RAND Corporation, 2012.

Elleman, Bruce A., Andrew Forbes, and David Rosenberg, eds. *Piracy and Maritime Crime Historical and Modern Case Studies.* Newport Papers ed. Vol. 35. Newport, RI: Naval War College Press, 2010.

Ghosh, PK. "Waiting to Explode: Piracy in the Gulf of Guinea." *Observer Research Foundation* Occasional Paper, no. 46 (September 2013): 1-34.

Gleick, James. *Chaos: Making a New Science.* New York, NY: Penguin Books, 1988.

Hansen, Stig Jarle. "Piracy in the Greater Gulf of Aden: Myths, Misconceptions and Remedies." *Norwegian Institute for Urban and Regional Research* 29 (2009), https://www.cimicweb.org/cmo/Piracy/Documents/Security/Piracy%20in%20the%20greater%20Gulf%20of%20Aden.pdf (accessed September 27, 2013).

Hastings, Justin V. "Geographies of State Failure and Sophistication in Maritime Piracy Hijackings." *Political Geography* 28, no. 4 (5, 2009): 213-23.

Haywood, Robert and Roberta Spivak. *Maritime Piracy.* New York, NY: Routledge, 2012.

Holland, John H. *Emergence: From Chaos to Order.* Reading, MA: Helix Books, Addison-Wesley, 1998.

———. *Hidden Order: How Adaptation Builds Complexity.* Reading, MA: Perseus Books, 1996.

International Chamber of Shipping. *BMP4: Best Management Practices for Protection Against Somalia Based Piracy.* Edinburgh, Scotland, UK: Witherby Publishing Group Limited, 2011.

Jablonski, Ryan S. and Steven Oliver. "The Political Economy of Plunder: Economic Opportunity and Modern Piracy." *Journal of Conflict Resolution* 57, no. 4 (August 01, 2013): 682-708, http://jcr.sagepub.com/content/57/4/682 (accessed November 15, 2013).

Johnson, George. *Fire in the Mind: Science, Faith, and the Search for Order.* New York, NY: Vintage Books, 1996.

Liss, Carolin. "New Actors and the State: Addressing Maritime Security Threats in Southeast Asia." *Contemporary Southeast Asia: A Journal of International and Strategic Affairs* 35, no. 2 (2013): 141-62 (accessed October 02, 2013).

Little, Benerson. *Pirate Hunting: The Fight Against Pirates, Privateers, and Sea Raiders from Antiquity to the Present.* Washington, DC: Potomac Books, 2010.

McKnight, Terry and Michael Hirsh. *Pirate Alley: Commanding Task Force 151 Off Somalia.* Annapolis, MD: Naval Institute Press, 2012.

Nincic, Donna. "Maritime Piracy in Africa: The Humanitarian Dimension." *African Security Studies* 18, no. 3 (2009): 1-16.

Payne, John C. *Piracy Today: Fighting Villainy on the High Seas.* Dobbs Ferry, NY: Sheridan House, 2010.

Stavridis, James. "Pirate Droves: How to Deal with Ransom on the High Seas." *Foreign Policy.* November 07, 2013. http://www.foreignpolicy.com/articles/2013/11/07/pirate_droves_stavridis (accessed November 08, 2013).

Sunvold, Daniel D. "Concept of Operations for a Self-Organizing Theater Ballistic Missile Defense Network." MS, Naval Postgraduate School, Monterey, CA, 1999.

Toland, Ronald W. "A Maritime Approach to Countering Horn of Africa Piracy." MS, National Defense University, Joint Forces Staff College, Joint Advanced Warfighting School, Norfolk, VA, 2012.

Vego, Milan. "Counter-Piracy: An Operational Perspective." *Reprinted from Tidskrift i Sjövӓsendet*, no. 3 (2009): 169-80 (accessed July 30, 2013).

Vreÿ, Francois. "Bad Order at Sea: From the Gulf of Aden to the Gulf of Guinea." *African Security Studies* 18, no. 3 (2009): 17-30.

Walker, Timothy. "Maritime Security in West Africa: Aiming for Long-Term Solutions." *African Security Review* 22, no. 2 (2013): 85-91.

Yousef, Deena K. and Gismatullin, Eduard. "Kenya Attack Stirs Complacency Fear Over
    Somali Pirates." Bloomberg News. http://www.bloomberg.com/news/2013-09-
    25/kenya-attack-stirs-complacency-fear-over-somali-pirates.html (accessed October
    03, 2013).

Zacks, Richard. *The Pirate Coast: Thomas Jefferson, the First Marines, and the Secret
    Mission of 1805.* New York, NY: Hyperion, 2005.

www.ingramcontent.com/pod-product-compliance
Lightning Source LLC
Chambersburg PA
CBHW080536290526
45790CB00006B/2425